The Mind of A Child

Written by Miyonda Carter

Illustrated by China M. Harris

This line of children books are specially dedicated to my children, Precious Roundtree, Hollee Anderson, Marcus Morgan Jr., Markevious Morgan, and Marquis Morgan (Q). My Grandchildren, Kayden Anderson, Sariya Jones, Kaleb Anderson and the many more who are to come.

This is where legacy begins.

A good man leaves an inheritance to his children's children... Proverbs 13:22

Momma It's Gonna Be Alright!!

Meet Kayden

Momma it's gonna be alright don't cry anymore.
Momma it's gonna be alright I'll open and hold your door.

I'll help you make up your bed before I go to school.

I may not can cook right now, but I'll help you take off your shoes.
After a long day at work Momma I'm so glad that you are home.

I didn't answer the knock at the door today before you got home. I locked the door behind me and went straight to my room.

Momma I studied my sight words and I can now spell broom.
Momma I don't mind eating from Mickey D's again.
Momma it's gonna be alright I promise to be your friend.

What was Kayden's sight word?
Do you remember what color it was written in?
Can you spell it out loud?

The memory of the righteous is blessed...
Proverbs 10:7 (New King James Version)

The Tooth Fairy Forgot About Me!!

Meet Sariya

The Tooth Fairy forgot about me.
And I woke up wondering how can this be?

No dollars!? No change!? No note to even try to explain!?
Sitting there under my pillow where I left it was my tooth.
And I have no need of it because for months it's been loose.

Causing me problems every time I would try to eat,
I was so sure the tooth fairy would find it while I was fast asleep.

I was praying I'd get enough money to buy me a game.

I guess I better tell my mom and dad that the tooth fairy never came.

Let's use our imagination to talk about Sariya and her parent's conversation! How do you think Sariya felt when she realized her tooth was still under her pillow?

Please listen and answer me. Let me speak to you and tell you what upsets me.
Psalm 55:2 (ERV)

Q's New School!!

Meet Q and Kaleb

Q's family has moved and he's not very excited about starting a new school. He left all his friends back at home. So now he feels all alone.

On his way to school he's worried about what he will say.
He's also worried about having no friends at play.

He's been praying to God at night on his knees.
Asking him to supply all of his needs.

When he gets to his classroom he yells No Way!!
He sees one of his old friends from back in the day.

At recess they grab the basketball and head out to shoot hoops.
While on the way to play he tells God Thank You!

What did Q remember to do when he was feeling sad and confused?
What can you do when you find yourself feeling sad and blue?

My God shall supply all your need according to his riches in glory
forever and ever.
Philippians 4:19 (New King James Version)

WestBow Press books may be ordered through booksellers or by contacting:

WestBow Press
A Division of Thomas Nelson & Zondervan
1663 Liberty Drive
Bloomington, IN 47403
www.westbowpress.com
1 (866) 928-1240

ISBN: 978-1-9736-6772-8 (sc)
ISBN: 978-1-9736-6773-5 (e)

Library of Congress Control Number: 2019908818

Print information available on the last page.

WestBow Press rev. date: 7/9/2019

WESTBOW
P R E S S®
A DIVISION OF THOMAS NELSON
& ZONDERVAN

Printed in the United States
By Bookmasters